VINTAGE TRAVEL POSTERS
Make Your Own Art Masterpiece

Publisher and Creative Director: Nick Wells
Art Director: Mike Spender
Editorial: Laura Bulbeck
Illustrator: David Jones
Colours: Federica Ciaravella

FLAME TREE PUBLISHING
6 Melbray Mews
Fulham, London SW6 3NS
United Kingdom

www.flametreepublishing.com

First published 2018

18 20 22 21 19
1 3 5 7 9 10 8 6 4 2

A CIP record for this book is available from the British Library upon request.

ISBN 978-1-78664-790-0

Printed in China

VINTAGE TRAVEL POSTERS
Make Your Own Art Masterpiece

Illustrated by David Jones

Selected by Daisy Seal

FLAME TREE
PUBLISHING

Here are some of the hues used in this book. Use these as a starting point for your own art masterpieces.

Vintage Travel Posters

Throughout history, posters have been used to advertise anything from products to stage shows, exhibitions to travel, as well as being effective methods of propaganda. Vintage posters have now become works of art in their own right, and are hugely popular today due to the sense of nostalgia they evoke.

It is generally accepted that posters in the Art Nouveau period were the first in the category of 'art posters', when aspects of typography and design layout were as important as content. This was in part due to the development of printing technology, but also the realization by commercial organizations of the importance of effective communication to their consumers. As Art Deco developed as a popular art movement in the 1920s, its influence can clearly be seen in the stylized form of the travel posters produced during that time.

Travel posters were mostly developed by rail lines and airline companies – bursts of colour depicting charming landscapes and people making happy memories enticed viewers to go on a new adventure. The poster's role evolved from message medium to lifestyle communicator: presenting consumers with an identifiable aura that promised the excitement of a modern era.

Illustration based on travel poster for Japan, 1930s

Autumn: Red Leaves at Yunoyama Onsen

See the full poster online

flametr.com/vintage-travel

Vintage Travel Posters

MAKE YOUR OWN ART MASTERPIECE

Illustration based on travel poster for Japan, 1930s

Summer at Miho Peninsula

See the full poster online

flametr.com/vintage-travel

Vintage Travel Posters

MAKE YOUR OWN ART MASTERPIECE

Illustration based on travel poster for Japan, 1930s

Japan

See the full poster online

flametr.com/vintage-travel

Illustration based on travel poster for Algeria, c. 1910–59

Algérie

See the full poster online

flametr.com/vintage-travel

Illustration based on travel poster for China, *c.* 1930

Beauty and Grandeur – The Yangtsze Gorges in the Heart of China Will Amaze and Thrill You!

See the full poster online

flametr.com/vintage-travel

Vintage Travel Posters

MAKE YOUR OWN ART MASTERPIECE

Illustration based on travel poster for the Bahamas

Nassau

See the full poster online

flametr.com/vintage-travel

Illustration based on travel poster for England, 1924

Brightest London is Best Reached by Underground

See the full poster online

flametr.com/vintage-travel

Illustration based on travel poster for the USA, *c.* 1910–59

Chicago

See the full poster online

flametr.com/vintage-travel

Vintage Travel Posters

MAKE YOUR OWN ART MASTERPIECE

Illustration based on travel poster for Japan, 1930s

Come to Tokyo

See the full poster online

flametr.com/vintage-travel

Illustration based on travel poster for Italy, *c.* 1920

Cortina d'Ampezzo

See the full poster online

flametr.com/vintage-travel

Vintage Travel Posters

MAKE YOUR OWN ART MASTERPIECE

Illustration based on travel poster for Eastern Europe, 1935

Crimea

See the full poster online

flametr.com/vintage-travel

Illustration based on travel poster for Puerto Rico, *c.* 1936–40

Discover Puerto Rico, USA – Where the Americas Meet

See the full poster online

flametr.com/vintage-travel

Vintage Travel Posters

MAKE YOUR OWN ART MASTERPIECE

Illustration based on travel poster for Switzerland

Switzerland

See the full poster online

flametr.com/vintage-travel

Illustration based on travel poster for Egypt

Egypt

See the full poster online

flametr.com/vintage-travel

Illustration based on travel poster for England, 1908

Golders Green – A Place of Delightful Prospects

See the full poster online

flametr.com/vintage-travel

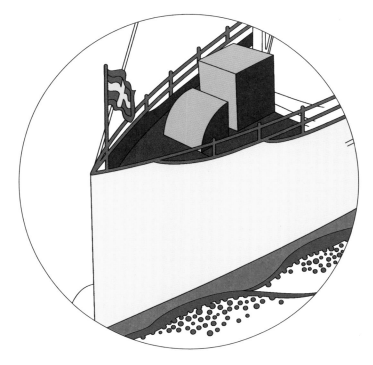

Illustration based on travel poster for Sweden, c. 1910–59

Sweden's Scenic Waterway – Göta Canal

See the full poster online

flametr.com/vintage-travel

Vintage Travel Posters

MAKE YOUR OWN ART MASTERPIECE

Illustration based on travel poster for the USA

Grand Staircase-Escalante National Monument, Utah

See the full poster online

flametr.com/vintage-travel

Vintage Travel Posters

MAKE YOUR OWN ART MASTERPIECE

Illustration based on travel poster for Italy, *c.* 1930

Italian Lakes

See the full poster online

flametr.com/vintage-travel

Illustration based on travel poster for Japan, *c.* 1912

Japan Tourist Bureau

See the full poster online

flametr.com/vintage-travel

Illustration based on travel poster for England, 1930s

Brighton Railway for Isle of Wight

See the full poster online

flametr.com/vintage-travel

Illustration based on travel poster for Italy, *c.* 1920

Milano

See the full poster online

flametr.com/vintage-travel

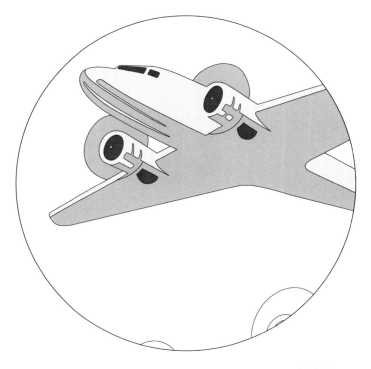

Illustration based on travel poster for the USA, 1936–37

City of New York Municipal Airports

See the full poster online

flametr.com/vintage-travel

Vintage Travel Posters

MAKE YOUR OWN ART MASTERPIECE

Illustration based on travel poster for New Zealand, 1927

Hanmer Springs

See the full poster online

flametr.com/vintage-travel

Vintage Travel Posters

MAKE YOUR OWN ART MASTERPIECE

Illustration based on travel poster for Japan, *c. 1893–1939*

Osaka Mercantile Steamship Co., Ltd

See the full poster online

flametr.com/vintage-travel

Vintage Travel Posters

MAKE YOUR OWN ART MASTERPIECE

Illustration based on travel poster for Peru, *c.* 1930–59

Peru of the Incas

See the full poster online

flametr.com/vintage-travel

Vintage Travel Posters

MAKE YOUR OWN ART MASTERPIECE

Illustration based on travel poster for England, 1915

Godstone

See the full poster online

flametr.com/vintage-travel

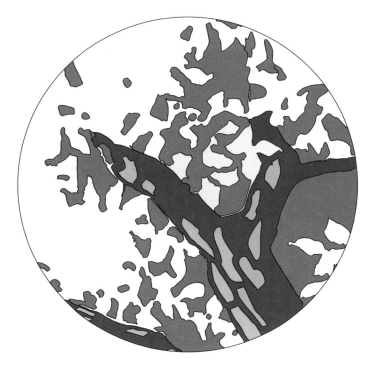

Illustration based on travel poster for England, 1915

Oxhey Woods

See the full poster online

flametr.com/vintage-travel

Vintage Travel Posters

MAKE YOUR OWN ART MASTERPIECE

Illustration based on travel poster for England, 1915

The North Downs

See the full poster online

flametr.com/vintage-travel

Vintage Travel Posters

MAKE YOUR OWN ART MASTERPIECE

Illustration based on travel poster for the USA, *c.* 1935

Pueblos of the Southwest

See the full poster online

flametr.com/vintage-travel

Illustration based on travel poster for Canada, 1945

The Royal York, Toronto, Canada

See the full poster online

flametr.com/vintage-travel

Vintage Travel Posters

MAKE YOUR OWN ART MASTERPIECE

Illustration based on travel poster for the USA, *c. 1936–40*

Rural Pennsylvania

See the full poster online

flametr.com/vintage-travel

Illustration based on travel poster for the USA, *c.* 1936–39

See America

See the full poster online

flametr.com/vintage-travel

Illustration based on travel poster for the USA, *c.* 1936–39

See America

See the full poster online

flametr.com/vintage-travel

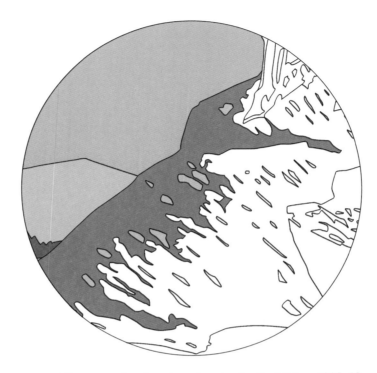

Illustration based on travel poster for the USA, *c. 1936–39*

The National Parks Preserve Wild Life

See the full poster online

flametr.com/vintage-travel

Vintage Travel Posters

MAKE YOUR OWN ART MASTERPIECE

Illustration based on travel poster for India

India

See the full poster online

flametr.com/vintage-travel

Illustration based on travel poster for the USA

San Francisco

See the full poster online

flametr.com/vintage-travel

Vintage Travel Posters

MAKE YOUR OWN ART MASTERPIECE

Illustration based on travel poster for Italy, *c.* 1920

Venice

See the full poster online

flametr.com/vintage-travel

Illustration based on travel poster for Italy, *c.* 1920

Venice and the Lido

See the full poster online

flametr.com/vintage-travel

Illustration based on travel poster for France

Fontainebleau

See the full poster online

flametr.com/vintage-travel

Vintage Travel Posters

MAKE YOUR OWN ART MASTERPIECE

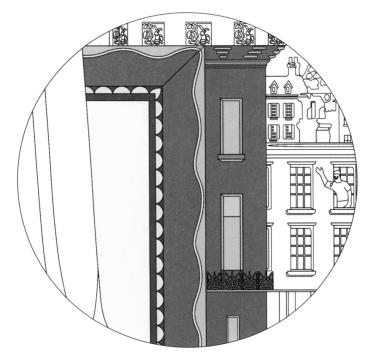

Illustration based on travel poster for France

Paris

See the full poster online

flametr.com/vintage-travel

Illustration based on travel poster for France

Paris

See the full poster online

flametr.com/vintage-travel

Vintage Travel Posters

MAKE YOUR OWN ART MASTERPIECE

Illustration based on travel poster for India, *c.* 1920

A Street by Moonlight – Visit India

See the full poster online

flametr.com/vintage-travel

Vintage Travel Posters

MAKE YOUR OWN ART MASTERPIECE

Illustration based on travel poster for Indonesia, *c. 1910–59*

Visit Java – Only 36 Hours from Singapore

See the full poster online

flametr.com/vintage-travel

Vintage Travel Posters

MAKE YOUR OWN ART MASTERPIECE

Illustration based on travel poster for the USA, 1936

Visit the Brookfield Zoo, Chicago, Illinois

See the full poster online

flametr.com/vintage-travel

Vintage Travel Posters

MAKE YOUR OWN ART MASTERPIECE

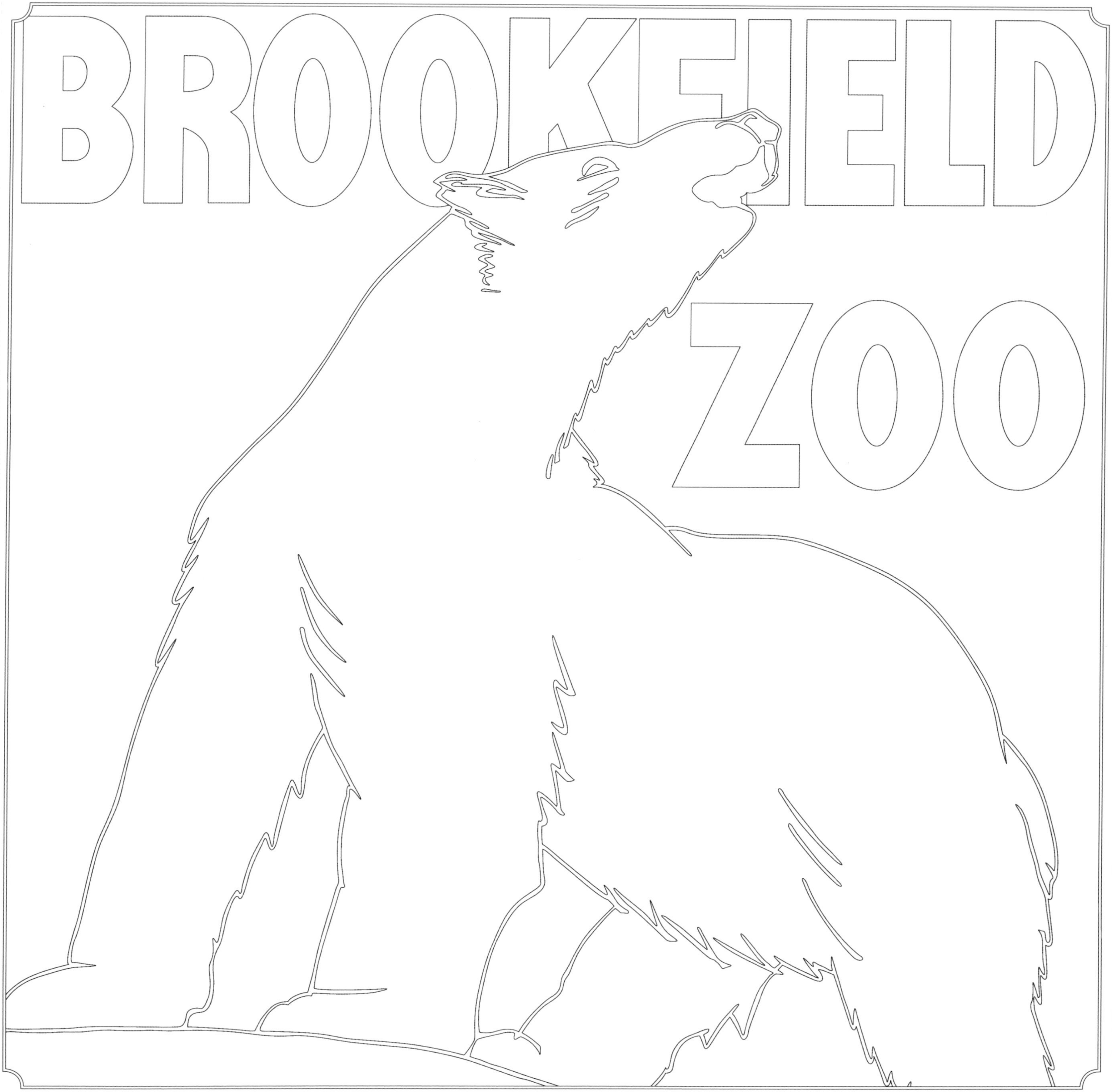
BROOKFIELD
ZOO

Illustration based on travel poster for Russia, 1932

Volga

See the full poster online

flametr.com/vintage-travel

For further illustrated books on a wide range of

art subjects, in various formats, please look at our website:

www.flametreepublishing.com